Tipper GORE

Tipper GORE

VOICE for the VOICELESS

JoAnn Bren Guernsey

Lerner Publications Company ■ Minneapolis

ACKNOWLEDGMENTS

AP/Wide World Photos, 11, 22, 23, 26, 33, 41, 42, 46, 50, 51, 53, 56, 57, 64; Harry Benson, 43, front cover; Tipper Gore, 12, 15; Carol Guzy/Washington Post, 55, 58, 63; Nashville Banner, 18 (bottom), 20; Official White House Photographs, 2, 60, back cover; Kathy Raskob/IPS, 28, 34; Reuters/Bettmann, 10, 49, 52, 61; UPI/Bettmann, 38; Day Walters/Day Walters Photographic Illustration, 25 (top); Eddie West/Carthage Courier, 18 (top), 35, 36 (top); Wide World Photos, Inc., 6; Larry Wilson/Kennedy Center at Peabody College, Vanderbilt University, 25 (bottom), 44.

This book is available in two bindings:
Library binding by Lerner Publications Company
Soft cover by First Avenue Editions
241 First Avenue North
Minneapolis, MN 55401

LIBRARY OF CONGRESS CATALOGING-IN-PUBLICATION DATA

Guernsey, JoAnn Bren.
Tipper Gore : a voice for the voiceless / JoAnn Bren Guernsey.
p.   cm. — (The Achievers)
Summary: Traces the life of Tipper Gore, wife of Vice President Al Gore, from birth through the early days of the Clinton administration.
ISBN 0-8225-2876-2 (lib. bdg.)
ISBN 0-8225-9651-2 (pbk.)
1. Gore, Tipper, 1948-   —Juvenile literature. 2. Gore, Albert, 1948-   —Juvenile literature. 3. Vice-Presidents' wives—United States—Biography—Juvenile literature. [1. Gore, Tipper, 1948-   . 2. Vice-Presidents' wives.] I. Title. II. Series.
E840.8.G66G84 1994
973.929'092–dc20
[B]   93-8165
                                                                    CIP
                                                                    AC

Manufactured in the United States of America

1 2 3 4 5 6 – P/JR – 99 98 97 96 95 94

Contents

1
"Skylark"

Tipper Gore had never felt so alone. She was exhausted by the day's events and stranded by a fierce storm at La Guardia Airport in New York. All flights to Washington, D.C., where her family awaited her, had been canceled. In her mind, Tipper kept replaying the hostile confrontation she had just experienced. For three hours, she had been verbally attacked by angry rock stars and other recording artists. To them Tipper was the enemy—a prudish fanatic who hated rock music and wanted to squash the free expression of artists everywhere. How, she wondered, could anyone think of her that way?

The National Association of Recording Arts and Sciences (NARAS—the organization that presents the Grammy Awards each year) had assembled a panel to discuss the issue of explicitly sexual and violent music lyrics. The NARAS had invited Tipper Gore to participate because she was the cofounder of a nonprofit organization called Parents' Music Resource Center (PMRC). Since 1985 she had been a leader in the campaign against what she termed "porn rock" and had been asking for warning labels on records, tapes, and compact discs.

Tipper knew that many songwriters and performers in the NARAS disagreed with the views of the PMRC, but she felt that they didn't understand what she wanted. She was definitely *not* in favor of censorship. She wondered if the NARAS was aware of how concerned parents and other consumers were about certain music lyrics. Surely the record industry cared about consumers and young listeners, didn't they?

But she never got her message through to them. The panel and the audience were filled with people who had already made up their minds about Tipper Gore. Every question was aimed at her like an arrow. Many of the questions were extremely personal and insulting, especially those regarding her sexual activities with her husband, United States senator Al Gore.

It was clear that this particular panel and audience assumed that Tipper, a stay-at-home mother of four, was just a neurotic housewife who disliked sex. They believed that her attitude toward explicit lyrics was based on her inability to handle the idea of her own children ever exploring their own sexuality.

Tipper wondered how successful representatives of the entertainment industry could be so insensitive. She'd expected a debate—not personal attacks.

Nevertheless, when asked later if she would have accepted the invitation had she known that almost everyone who participated in the panel discussion would disagree with her, she answered "yes," as calmly as she could. "I am pleased to discuss the issue—and to exercise my First Amendment rights." The panel, perhaps the whole entertainment industry, had made the mistake of underestimating Tipper Gore. The issue of "porn rock" would not go away—and neither would Tipper.

Seven years later, on November 3, 1992, Tipper faced a much larger audience that was anything but hostile. She heard the cheers and witnessed the excitement of thousands of supporters in Little Rock, Arkansas. The crowd was celebrating the election of a new U.S. president, Bill Clinton, and a new vice president, Al Gore. As the two leaders smiled and waved to the crowd, their wives were not simply part of the background.

An unusually large part of Clinton's campaign had involved his wife, Hillary Rodham Clinton. A strong-willed, brilliant, and successful career woman, Hillary made it clear that she would not be a traditional First Lady, confined to hosting luncheons and standing at her husband's elbow. She would be the president's *partner.*

From left to right, Hillary Rodham Clinton, President-elect Bill Clinton, Vice President-elect Al Gore, and Tipper Gore celebrate their election victory in Little Rock, Arkansas, on November 3, 1992. *Opposite,* Hillary, *left,* and Tipper, *right,* display T-shirts that they were given in Coatesville, Pennsylvania—a town known for its steel production.

Tipper Gore's behavior had also been considered highly unusual for a political spouse. Her husband had frequently been warned during the late 1980s to distance himself from her controversial PMRC activities or risk political ruin. But during the 1992 presidential campaign, the Republican party had made "family values" a rallying cry. Many people thought that Hillary Clinton was too liberal, too feminist, too strong and competent. But what about Tipper?

It was difficult for Clinton-Gore opponents to find fault with this attractive, fun-loving woman, who wasn't just devoted to her own family, but had made the issue of "family values" a part of her life. Most people no longer viewed Tipper as a prudish, humorless, anti-music housewife. Instead she became a political asset.

10

What you see when you first meet Tipper Gore is an all-American beauty—vivacious, upbeat, and free-spirited. After her husband became vice president, the Secret Service, which guards the families of the president and vice president, gave Tipper the code name "Skylark." She seems to be the perfect wife and mom, driving her four children to endless activities, attending PTA (Parent-Teacher Association) meetings, and preparing family meals. But if you look closer you see much more.

Tipper is a skilled and experienced politician, having spent 16 years in the nation's capital. She became a good friend and partner to the First Lady, easily blending her form of activism with Hillary Rodham Clinton's. Together they quickly demonstrated a deep commitment to issues involving children, women, and the disadvantaged.

2
From Childhood to Motherhood

Mary Elizabeth Aitcheson was born in Washington, D.C., on August 19, 1948. The nickname *Tipper* came from a lullaby her mother often sang to her daughter, an only child who remembers often feeling lonely.

Tipper's mother, Margaret Odom, married John Aitcheson in 1947, after her first husband had been killed in World War II. When Tipper was two years old, however, her parents divorced. "The marriage was a mistake," her mother says, "except for Tipper."

Mother and daughter then moved in with Tipper's grandparents, who lived in Arlington, Virginia, a suburb of Washington, D.C. Her grandfather, a prominent banker, had built the house in 1938.

Tipper attended Saint Agnes, a private girls' school in Alexandria, Virginia. She describes herself as an average student who especially loved history and music. But much of her spare time was devoted to sports. She played basketball in the winter, softball in the spring, and she was captain of her field hockey team during the summer. Although outgoing and talkative, Tipper also enjoyed solitary activities such as climbing trees, playing in her tree house, reading, and collecting tadpoles and other small animals. She named one pet tree frog De Gaulle, after the French president. Tipper and a group of friends established a book club in which they pooled their books and checked them out, as they would have done in a library.

Not all of her childhood memories are pleasant, however. At school, classmates often teased Tipper because she came from a "broken home." Divorce was not common in the 1950s and was often a source of shame for the people involved. Although Tipper says she now has a good relationship with her father (a Washington, D.C., businessman), during her childhood she saw him only on Sundays.

Being teased for "having no father" made Tipper feel different from her peers. However, these feelings increased her understanding of other people and contributed to her activism in later life on behalf of the homeless, the mentally ill, and children. "Growing up with divorce is not easy," she says. "But it has given me empathy for people who might be going through less-than-perfect lives."

Contrary to what people said about her during her campaign against porn rock, Tipper has always loved music. In high school, she played the drums in an all-girl rock band called the Wildcats. She still has her old drum set in the basement of her Virginia home.

When she was 16 years old, Tipper's life changed forever. She attended a senior prom at Saint Albans, an exclusive prep school in Washington, D.C. There she met 17-year-old Albert Gore, Jr. Al was the only son of Senator Albert Gore, a powerful Democratic legislator from Tennessee. Young Al was already quite sure that his future would also be in politics.

Family friends Trina and Esther Martin sit on either side of Tipper at her home in Arlington, Virginia. The dog's name is Bitsy.

When asked about the couple's first encounter at the prom, Tipper replies, "absolutely pure animal magnetism." She was "pleased but not surprised" when Al called her the next day for a date. They went to a party, and she remembers "dancing and dancing. Suddenly there was just the two of us; everybody else melted away." Al broke off his previous romance with his childhood sweetheart and turned his attention instead to Tipper.

It wasn't long before Al invited her to meet his family on their large farm in Carthage, Tennessee. Al's father vividly remembers this first meeting with Tipper. "She was dressed fit to kill. She was a lovely blonde, beautiful sparkling eyes, shapely and pleasant. I was even more struck by her beauty the next morning. She came to breakfast with every eyelash in place. She was dressed for an evening ball."

In 1966, about a year later, Al went to Harvard University, just outside of Boston, Massachusetts. After graduating from high school in 1967, Tipper attended nearby Boston University, where her political and social activism began. During the 1960s, many college campuses were in a state of turbulence. The opinion of people in the United States was divided about American involvement in the Vietnam War. Race riots tore many cities apart. Leaders with messages of hope and peace—such as President John F. Kennedy, civil rights leader Martin Luther King, Jr., and Robert F. Kennedy (who was seeking the Democratic nomination for president)—were assassinated. Along with many of her classmates, Tipper marched in demonstrations against the war and in support of civil rights.

At the end of her junior year, Al officially asked Tipper to marry him, and she quickly accepted. "We had gone out to dinner and we were walking by the Charles River," she recalls. "He had this beautiful ring. It was a very romantic proposal."

Soon after Al graduated from Harvard in 1969, he enlisted in the army. Tipper graduated from Boston University in 1970 with a degree in psychology.

A month after her graduation, they were married, and Tipper joined Al in Daleville, Alabama, near his army base. They lived modestly in a trailer park and worried about Al being sent to Vietnam. But they nonetheless shared a wonderful first year together. "It was great," Tipper says. "We were newly married, we were in love, it was fabulous."

On Christmas Day 1971, Al left for Vietnam. Although he worked as an army journalist rather than as a combat soldier, Tipper still worried about him. "It was a rough time," she admits. "The war was raging. Al's father had just been defeated in a very nasty senatorial election (largely because of his opposition to the war), Nixon was president. It was all very depressing."

Top, the Gore home in Elmwood, Tennessee, a community just outside of Carthage. *Bottom, from left to right:* Senator Albert Gore, Sr., Al, Karenna, and Tipper Gore in Carthage.

18

Al was in Vietnam for about six months. When he returned home, he studied religion and law at Vanderbilt University in Nashville, Tennessee, and worked as a newspaper reporter for the *Tennessean*. Tipper worked at the *Tennessean* too, as a part-time photographer. She was also pursuing a master's degree in psychology at George Peabody College, now a part of Vanderbilt University. In August 1973, when Tipper gave birth to their first child, Karenna, she had to divide her time between her baby and her studies. She received her degree in 1975, not knowing the challenges she would face in the future.

Tipper stood beside Al as he announced that he would run for Congress in 1976.

3
Entering the Political Arena

When Tipper married Al Gore, she entered a life of politics and strong family ties. His father, Albert, Sr., served three terms in the U.S. Senate, and his mother, Pauline, was among the first women ever to receive a law degree from Vanderbilt University. Both parents expected great things from their son, but Mrs. Gore denies having programmed Al for politics. "We brought him up to do a good job in whatever he chose to do," she says. But for years, politics was a powerful force in the Gore family. Al's only sister, Nancy, (10 years older than he) helped run their father's campaigns. When Al began his political career, Nancy became one of his most trusted advisers.

Al Gore first ran for public office in 1976, at age 27. He was running for a vacant congressional seat.

Tipper, an avid photographer, took pictures during the 1993 presidential campaign, as a Secret Service agent looked on, *left.* The photographs were shown later at an exhibit at the Smithsonian's National Museum of American Art in Washington, D.C., *opposite.*

On the day he announced his candidacy, he was so nervous that he threw up in the men's room in the Carthage courthouse. He did, however, go on to win the election. The Gores moved their young family into Tipper's childhood home in Arlington. But during Al's 16 years in Congress (8 years each in the House and the Senate), they shuttled back and forth between Arlington and Carthage, where they had a farm next to that of Al's parents.

Tipper had to be strong and ambitious just to stay out of the imposing shadow cast by the other Gore women. Her mother-in-law, for example, bought all of Tipper's clothes, until Al insisted that she stop. Tipper worked hard and efficiently during Al's campaigns, including that first 1976 race, during which she was pregnant with their second child.

The demands made on Tipper by both family and politics did not stop her from pursuing her own interests with enthusiasm and determination. "I built a darkroom at my home in Virginia and free-lanced in Washington," she says. The *Washington Star* and the *Washington Post* both published her photos, as did several trade journals. She insisted on working as a freelancer so she could set her own schedule. "I had young children," she points out.

The couple had always dreamed of having a large family, partly because they both had grown up wishing for the closeness of brothers and sisters. They settled for four children—Karenna, Kristin, Sarah, and Albert III. Tipper sees the size of her family as a compromise. "It's kind of hard to give up. I loved being pregnant and having the children."

She denies sacrificing her own ambitions as a psychologist or a photographer for her family or for Al's career. "If I'd wanted to go for my own career and get somebody to take care of the children, I would have done that. I truly did not wish to. I wanted to spend a lot of time with our kids. I'm having an impact in a different way."

One of those ways evolved during the mid-1980s, when Tipper became an ardent volunteer for several causes. Her children all played roles in determining the nature of Tipper's volunteer work. Two of her causes, in fact, sprang from conversations with her daughters. One afternoon while driving home with the children, the girls pointed out a filthy woman—dressed in rags, and talking to herself—standing on a corner near the Capitol.

"Can we help her?" they asked. "Can we take her home with us?" Tipper explained why they couldn't take the woman home. Then she and her children made the decision to volunteer some of their time to shelters for the homeless and the mentally ill.

In 1992 the National Mental Health Association presented Tipper with its first Remember the Children Award, *top*. Preschool children sent Tipper a thank-you card after she visited their class. Dr. Susan Gray, credited as the inspiration for the Head Start program, admires the children's handiwork.

Grappling with lumber, Tipper helps construct a house with other volunteers from Habitat for Humanity — a group that builds houses for the poor and the homeless.

Tipper went on to organize a group called Families for the Homeless that helped raise money and public consciousness about the issue. Working with the National Mental Health Association (NMHA), she also organized a major photographic exhibit entitled "Homeless in America: A Photographic Project." The exhibit, which depicted the plight of the nation's homeless, opened at the Corcoran Gallery in Washington, D.C., in 1988 and toured the country for two years.

Tipper's work on behalf of needy people continued. As founder of Tennessee Voices for Children, she established a coalition to promote the development of services for children and youth with serious behavioral, emotional, substance abuse, or other mental health problems. She also served as cochair of the Child Mental Health Interest Group, a nonpartisan group established by the NMHA.

In 1992 the NMHA presented Tipper with its first Remember the Children Award for her years of work on behalf of America's children. In 1993 the award was renamed. It is now the Tipper Gore Remember the Children Award, and it is presented by her at the organization's annual meetings.

Besides her voluntary work for the homeless and mentally ill, Tipper soon got deeply entrenched in another battle—this time against what she called "porn rock." And this battle made Tipper Gore a household name.

4
Battling an X-Rated Society

Like many parents of my generation, I grew up listening to rock music and loving it, watching television and being entertained by it. I still enjoy both. But something has happened since the days of "Twist and Shout" and "I Love Lucy."

...A small but immensely successful minority of performers have pioneered the "porn rock" phenomenon [which] is only part of an escalating trend toward the use of more explicit sex and graphic violence in entertainment industry offerings from movies and videos to jeans and perfume ads.

...In the course of my work, I've encountered a degree of callousness toward children that I never imagined existed. No one asks what is the product or its effect on kids, only how well it will sell.

—Tipper Gore, from the introduction to
Raising PG Kids in an X-Rated Society

In December 1984, Tipper purchased Prince's best-selling album *Purple Rain* for her 11-year-old daughter, Karenna. When she brought it home, she and Karenna listened to the album. The explicitly sexual lyrics embarrassed them both.

At about the same time, her two younger daughters, ages six and eight, began questioning their mother about frightening things they'd seen on MTV. Tipper sat down with them and watched music videos that featured such images as nearly naked women being captured and caged by the male rock stars, and a dead woman tied up with barbed wire.

Tipper got angry. She called her good friend Susan Baker, the wife of James Baker (who became President George Bush's secretary of state in 1989). Together with a few other well-connected and concerned friends, Tipper established a nonprofit organization called the Parents' Music Resource Center. In mid-1985 this group set out to alert other parents in their community—and eventually across the nation—to the emergence of what they called "porn rock." The group hoped to raise public awareness of the issue, generate discussion, and begin a constructive dialogue with people in the entertainment industry.

The PMRC decided that most parents simply didn't know about the recent trends in rock music, and if they did know, they didn't know what to do about it. The PMRC developed a simple strategy—to expose the most offensive song lyrics and videos to the public. And it worked. Parents became outraged when they heard and saw their children's rock heroes glamorize and even appear to encourage rape, torture, incest, suicide, and murder.

"Porn rock" quickly became a national issue. Newspapers and magazines printed articles that were, for the most part, supportive of the PMRC. Tipper and other group leaders were flooded with requests to appear on radio and television news and talk shows to discuss porn rock and what could be done about it.

By August 1985, however, representatives of the record industry began to fight back, accusing the PMRC of promoting censorship. Tipper continued to claim that the PMRC approach was the opposite of censorship, since members of the organization were attempting to *increase* information—not suppress it. They did not call for a ban of any album, no matter how offensive. But PMRC members did suggest ways that consumers could be warned about lyrics through the use of labels on albums, tapes, and compact discs. They also suggested that lyrics be printed and easily visible on the outside packaging.

Who would decide what was offensive and what would require warning labels? The PMRC said that the music industry itself should take that responsibility, since it had allowed the situation to develop in the first place.

By this time, many members of the United States Congress had begun to take an interest in the issue, and they decided to hold hearings (special meetings) on it. Senator John Danforth of Missouri was the chairman of the Senate's commerce committee, which is in charge of communications issues. In September 1985, he held a hearing to determine how widespread so-called porn rock really was and what effect it had on children. Unfortunately for Tipper, her husband, Al, was a member of the commerce committee, and this made it seem as though she were using her position unfairly. But she insisted that this was "my thing, not my husband's. I was an activist before I married him. This is not the wife of a senator who has suddenly gone nuts."

Both sides of the porn rock issue were well represented at the commerce committee hearing. Tipper and Susan Baker testified, as did representatives from the national PTA. Recording artists Frank Zappa, John Denver, and Dee Snider (of the band Twisted Sister) also spoke before the committee. The hearing turned out to be one of the most widely publicized in congressional history, and it brought the issue out for public debate.

The hearing did not resolve the porn rock issue, but it did call for further negotiations. The end result was a compromise that most people felt was workable and fair.

During September 1985, Tipper testified on Capitol Hill before the Senate Commerce Committee. She spoke about rock music lyrics that she considered offensive.

TIPPER GORE

RAISING PG KIDS IN AN X RATED SOCIETY

EXPLICIT MATERIAL— PARENTAL ADVISORY

WHAT PARENTS CAN
DO TO PROTECT THEIR CHILDREN
FROM SEX AND VIOLENCE
IN THE MEDIA

In her book, Tipper proposes that record albums, cassettes, and compact discs be given warning labels similar to those used for movies.

Selected albums would have a warning that would read "Explicit Lyrics—Parental Advisory." In exchange for this label, the PMRC dropped some of its other requests and agreed to stop their media campaign for a full year. During that period of time, the success of the warning label could be evaluated.

Meanwhile, however, Tipper continued to be the victim of harsh attacks, and they were becoming more and more personal. Some critics dismissed the PMRC as a bunch of "Washington wives," and Tipper in particular was dubbed a "cultural terrorist." Writers for magazines such as *Penthouse* and *Hustler* called her names and speculated about her sexual relations with her husband.

Disregarding the pressure to pull back, however, she became even more visible in 1987. She published a book entitled *Raising PG Kids in an X-Rated Society*. In her book, she used many specific examples from actual recordings and videos, and she suggested having ratings for music much like those used for movies. Her book was well received, and she took time away from home to promote it all over the country.

From left to right: Sarah, Karenna, Kristin, and Tipper listen as Al announces that he will be a presidential candidate in 1988.

Tipper was the guest speaker at a fund-raiser during her husband's campaign to become the Democratic nominee for president.

In 1987, however, Al decided to run for president of the United States. Tipper canceled the rest of her book tour and divided her time between the campaign and her children. As it turned out, Al soon realized that he would not be nominated as the Democratic presidential candidate, so he dropped out of the race.

During this time, his political career appeared to be in trouble, and the amount of time he spent campaigning—away from his family—caused tension between him and Tipper. Their 1987 experiences in the political arena would have a dramatic effect on them both a few years later, when Al's career took a promising turn.

Meanwhile, celebrated author Tipper Gore enjoyed the success of her book. A paperback edition was published, and the book continues to reach a wide audience. It became clear that Tipper and the PMRC never intended to censor music lyrics or videotapes. They had found effective ways to prevent community feelings from being ignored, while also respecting the rights insured by the First Amendment.

Al responds to a question during a press conference as Tipper holds their son, Albert Gore III. The senator announced that he would no longer seek the Democratic presidential nomination.

5
The Accident

When Al Gore decided to run for the presidency in April 1987, he hadn't included Tipper in his decision. Friends say that she was furious. Something as major as a political campaign requires teamwork, and she wasn't sure a bid for the presidency was the best thing, at that time, for the young Gore family. Two years later, a tragedy occurred that convinced both Al and Tipper that family does comes first.

In April 1989, Al and his six-year-old son, Albert III, attended an Orioles baseball game. As they were leaving Memorial Stadium after the game, Albert suddenly darted away from his father and into the road. A car hit him and threw him 30 feet, nearly killing Albert. He was rushed, unconscious, to the hospital, where doctors found several bones broken and internal organs crushed.

Tipper joined Al at their son's bedside. When young Albert regained consciousness, he told his parents, "I can't get well without you." For the next several months, Al and Tipper rarely left his side. Even when they brought him home in a full body cast, they set up his bed in the dining room and put a mattress on the floor, so they could take turns sleeping next to him.

The ordeal of the accident and Albert's long, painful recovery led the Gore family to seek counseling. Al was feeling guilty, as though he should have been able to prevent the accident. Tipper was terrified, overly protective, and also somewhat angry—common emotions following a nearly fatal accident. When asked about the crisis counseling, she says, "Our marriage wasn't in trouble. Whenever a parent has a child injured, and particularly when you're with the child and you see it happen, you have tremendous guilt." They found the counseling extremely valuable in facing trauma that, as Tipper put it, "drops like a bomb."

Albert has since recovered from his serious injuries and is now even active in sports. But experiencing the accident altered the Gore family forever. "I think because of the time that we spent together," Tipper says, "we've become much stronger as a family." And Al and Tipper ended up with a different kind of partnership. They now act more as a team. Al Gore decided not to run for the presidency again in 1992.

Al and Tipper look over get-well cards sent to their son, Albert III, after his accident in April 1989.

To do so would have required a year of campaigning prior to the Democratic National Convention. His family would have been adversely affected by the long, strenuous campaign for the Democratic nomination. Ultimately the strengthening of Al and Tipper's personal relationship enhanced their political one as well.

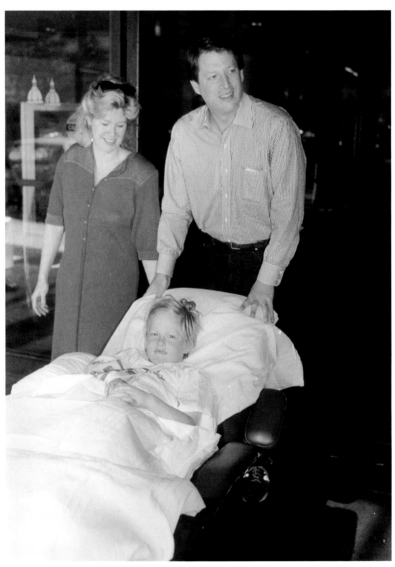

After more than three weeks in Johns Hopkins Hospital, Albert III gets to go home. Tipper and Al escort him.

Tipper relaxes in the family's Alexandria, Virginia, home.

However, Tipper's friends say that she did not recover immediately from Albert's accident and that it changed her for a while. One friend described her, at the time, as "beaten down, quieter, and not as assertive as she normally was." She did not throw herself into public life as much as she had before the accident. Tipper confided to some friends that she feels the accident, following so closely after Al's failed presidential bid, robbed the family of important time together before Karenna left for college. Another friend observed that Tipper took a long time to get back to her "jovial, fun-loving self."

Tipper carefully guards her family's privacy, shielding them from reporters and refusing to allow anyone to turn her children into political "props." And no matter how busy her schedule is, Tipper squeezes in as many family activities as possible, activities such as water-skiing, hiking, and—since Al gave her a pair of in-line skates for her 40th birthday—in-line skating.

Tipper Gore and Dr. Susan Gray admire the artwork of pre-schoolers at the Susan Gray School. Tipper was a member of the school's national advisory committee.

It's not uncommon to see Tipper attending, even presiding over public events, doing what she needs to do, then slipping out a side door as quickly as possible to help Albert with homework or drive one of her children somewhere. "I have a young family," she explains, "and I'm sure people understand."

The trauma of Albert's accident also made Tipper more aware of her need to take care of herself. She focused on exercise routines and on her eating habits. "It's not a diet," she insists. "It's a low-fat way of eating. Instead of snacking on chocolate-chip cookies, I have gingersnaps because they are low in fat and fulfill the need for something sweet." Besides in-line skating, her favorite forms of exercise include swimming at a nearby health club, walking, and running.

Whenever their hectic schedules permit, Tipper also runs (up to eight miles) with Al in the morning, soon after the children leave for school. They both value this time set aside not only for exercise but also to reinforce their already strong bond, which was especially important during the 1992 presidential campaign.

Vice President Al Gore and Tipper leave their limousine to walk down Pennsylvania Avenue and wave to the crowds watching the inaugural parade.

6
"Second" Lady

On July 7, 1992, at 11 P.M., the Gore family received a telephone call that would alter their lives forever. The call was not entirely unexpected. In fact, a group of reporters had gathered in the Gores' driveway in Carthage. They knew that Al was one of the people that Bill Clinton—then the Democratic presidential nominee—might choose to be his running mate.

The phone rang just as Tipper emerged from the shower. She picked up the receiver and heard Bill Clinton's distinctive voice, "Hi, Tipper. I hope I didn't wake you up, [but] if I did, I needed to." She told him they were all awake and then went to call Al to the phone. Yes, Bill Clinton definitely wanted Al as his vice presidential candidate. When the conversation ended, Tipper was "pleased, supportive, and excited."

They had discussed the situation at great length together. Family still came first for Al, but the campaign would last only three months. It would be shorter and less difficult than running for president. Besides, Tipper felt strongly from the beginning that Al's presence on the ticket would make it "a winning combination." She and Al had talked about the need for change in the United States, and how he and Bill Clinton as a team could "offer leadership toward a whole range of domestic goals we thought had been ignored."

No, the call from Bill Clinton was not exactly a surprise. Tipper remembers all the earlier, private meetings between Al and Bill and says that "the rapport between them was phenomenal. That's something we knew before Bill decided, that perhaps other people did not." Did she regret that her husband would not be the one running for president instead? "No, no, no," she says with conviction. "This is the way it should be. It all flowed from good decisions made for the right reasons."

Soon after Al accepted the vice presidential candidacy, Tipper Gore found a friend in Hillary Rodham Clinton. Tipper and Hillary had met previously at various political functions, but the first time they really got to know each other was when the Gore family went to Little Rock for the announcement of Al's candidacy. "They just hit it off really well, right away," says Vice President Gore. Both being mothers, they shared a strong concern about protecting their children and giving them as normal a life as possible.

From left to right: President Bill Clinton, Hillary Rodham Clinton, Chelsea Clinton, Kristin Gore, Sarah Gore, Al Gore III, Tipper Gore, and Vice President Al Gore wave to supporters in Little Rock, Arkansas.

"We are on the same wavelength, and I enjoy her," says Tipper. "Beyond that I respect and appreciate her and admire the way she has handled her life."

It was a good thing they got along so well, because they were about to spend enough time together to strain even the closest of friendships. For days and weeks on end, their husbands campaigned together.

Hillary and Tipper found themselves sharing not only bus seats and meals, but also the avid attention of reporters and Secret Service people. They also shared confidences.

"Just imagine," Tipper said during the campaign, "being two couples on a bus for four or five days. It's really been very intimate—*very intimate*. It's a major double date. We each have our own bus. We go to their bus. They come to ours. They come to lunch on our bus. They invite us to dinner. We all get together and just talk. I said one day, 'I know why this is so much fun; it reminds me of college.'"

Cuban-American labor leader Anita Cofino presents a bouquet of flowers to Tipper in Miami, Florida.

Tipper speaks to senior citizens in Laguna Hills, California, during the 1992 presidential campaign.

Hillary Rodham Clinton, *left,* smiles as Tipper gives the thumbs-up sign at an inaugural luncheon in January 1993.

At times during the campaign, Tipper (then 44) and Hillary (then 45) seemed like twins and were treated as such by the media. Their hair was almost the same length, style, and color. They both liked to wear tailored suits with long jackets and short skirts in similarly bright colors. They seemed to enjoy the same kind of humor and make similar comical faces at the media cameras, which never seemed to leave them alone. On stage, at the climax of the Democratic

National Convention in July, the two women grabbed each other in a spontaneous and lively dance to the campaign theme song, Fleetwood Mac's "Don't Stop Thinking about Tomorrow."

But their relationship is not just a political necessity. Tipper calls Hillary her "long-lost sister." And Hillary gives Tipper credit as "a real partner, somebody I can talk to, somebody who sees the world as I do."

A 19-month-old child snuggles in Tipper's arms during a dedication ceremony for a homeless center in the Bronx, New York. The child and her mother are residents of the center.

Often, while campaigning, Tipper would catch Hillary's eye and give her a wink or a supportive smile. This became especially helpful when the public and the media attacked Hillary as a "problem" during the campaign.

Tipper knew all too well what it felt like to receive public attacks and criticism for the kind of wife and mother—the kind of woman—she was. Her campaign against violent and sexual lyrics was still raised by some as proof that she would be an inappropriate "Second Lady."

"There are very few people who can understand what you're going through," says Chris Downey, whose husband was also in Congress. "Everyone thinks 'Oh, how glamorous, oh, how wonderful being a candidate's wife.' But those looks [that Hillary and Tipper exchange] are very comforting. It's nice to know that there's somebody there to help you through it. It's not like 'I think I know what you're going through.' It's 'I know I know what you're going through.'"

Several speakers at the Republican National Convention in August 1992 attacked Hillary Rodham Clinton for being a career woman. They even said that she represented "antifamily" values. One of Bill Clinton's aides says that Tipper was enraged by this attack and determined to defend Hillary. Natilee Duning, a Tennessee friend who has known Tipper for many years says, "When Tipper is your friend, she's your friend forever."

Tipper enjoys nature and a cup of coffee on the deck of the family's home in Virginia.

Hillary and Tipper admire and publicly praise each other. Hillary, known to be dedicated to issues involving children, often introduces Tipper to audiences as an advocate not only for children but also for the homeless and the mentally ill. And Tipper admits she loves hearing Hillary speak. Many people, in fact, believe Tipper has learned a lot from Hillary about making effective public appearances, especially when audiences are not entirely friendly. Occasionally Tipper is still booed by people because of her stand on music lyrics, but she says when that happens, it no longer upsets her.

She and Hillary do share a tendency to stand openly, unafraid, in the public eye. Both are impossible to ignore or dismiss. However, the two women are also very different from each other, and these differences go beyond the fact that one has a professional career and the other has worked primarily at home. For one thing, Tipper's personality makes her one of the easiest public figures to genuinely *like*, even in that most critical and combative of all places, the nation's capital. Both Republicans and Democrats praise Tipper Gore.

Her approach to the difficult 1992 presidential campaign was refreshingly cheerful. For example, Tipper did not take any of the attacks on her husband personally, because she understands politics. "If I have a good personal relationship with someone," she explains, "I can ignore any unpleasantness, just shrug it off.

During a 1992 rally just outside Cleveland, Ohio, Tipper hands the microphone to Hillary Rodham Clinton.

Tipper, *third from left,* examines part of the AIDS memorial quilt, which displays the names of and tributes to people who have died of the disease.

Many of Tipper's friends enjoy her sense of humor, and some of her jokes gained publicity during the presidential campaign.

I know it's said in the heat of battle." At least once, she responded to the constant presence of reporters by soaking them with a water pistol. Her most publicized joke, however, occurred one evening after several long hours of campaigning. Al was being interviewed on "Larry King Live," a television interview show that is broadcast live and allows people to call in with questions or comments.

Tipper and her staff had just checked in at a motel to watch the program, when she got a mischievous look in her eye. "Let's call in," she said to her press aide, KiKi Moore. After dialing the show's number and waiting several minutes for her call to get through, she lowered her voice and whispered, "Senator, I just had to tell you, you're the most handsome man I've ever seen." She then asked him for a date.

Al did not recognize her voice. The television audience watched as a dignified vice presidential candidate blushed and stammered until Larry King stepped in. He scolded the caller, reminding her that the senator was married and not about to make a date.

"Not even with his wife?" Tipper asked laughingly. She was surprised, the next day, by all the publicity her joke generated, but that did not cause her to change her style in the least.

Interviewed in her Virginia home shortly before she and her family were to move into the vice presidential mansion, she complained good-naturedly about the move. What she would miss the most was her darkroom, where she has developed all of her own black-and-white photographs. "I don't know what I'm going to do. Maybe I won't go," she joked. "Al will stay in the veep's house and I'll stay in our house and we'll get on great."

By that time, everyone knew what to expect from the new Second Lady. One political observer put it this way: "If you have your choice of dining with Bill or Hillary or Al or Tipper, pick Tipper. She's the most fun!"

Shortly after the election, Tipper resigned from the PMRC, which had accomplished what it set out to do. She decided to focus her energy on her other two areas of concern, mental health and homelessness. She also has the extra duties of being Second Lady.

Tipper is known for her work on behalf of children.

As part of the 1992 inaugural celebration, a group of celebrities performed on the steps of the Lincoln Memorial. *From left to right:* Tipper Gore, Vice President Al Gore, Albert Gore III, Hillary Rodham Clinton, Evelyn Ashford (of Ashford and Simpson), Stevie Wonder (behind unidentified woman), Michael Jackson, Chelsea Clinton, President Clinton, and Diana Ross.

When Tipper Gore and Hillary Rodham Clinton appeared at a luncheon for congressional spouses, Tipper was clearly at ease in the situation. A writer for *Good Housekeeping* magazine observed the two women and commented on the contrast in their styles.

While the First Lady appeared more "reserved and cool," greeting the guests at table after table, Tipper "swooped around the room with open arms, joking, laughing, hugging and kissing friends, and catching up on news of husbands and children."

When it was her turn to speak, Tipper stood at the podium without notes and reminisced about the campaign. She said it had been a team effort and "the most exciting and exhilarating experience of my life." She praised Hillary for her unwavering leadership and vision and offered a prediction. She said that the new First Lady was going to be "a rainbow of hope, a beacon for those who care for children and families." Later, the two women cheerfully embraced and Hillary referred to Tipper as the one person in Washington she could truly rely on.

Those who know the Second Lady best would certainly agree. This determined wife, mother, and activist has been assigned another role—perhaps her most challenging one yet—and she has found her own unique way to fill it.

Tipper Gore in her
White House office